Where Things Are

poems by

Joan Gibb Engel

Finishing Line Press
Georgetown, Kentucky

Where Things Are

ACKNOWLEDGMENTS

I am grateful to the editors of the following publications in which these poems
first appeared:

"After a Phone Call." *The Comstock Review*
"Cordless" *Blotter Magazine*
"A Drawerful of Meadowlarks." www.practicalethics.net and
        humansandnature.org
"Query." *Under a Warm Green Linden*
"Stereopsis." *San Pedro River Review*

Many thanks to the members of the Dry River Poets, especially our taskmaster
Sandy Szelag. These poems could not have been written without the stimulus
provided by teachers and poets associated with the Poetry Center of the
University of Arizona. Thank you to Randall Freisinger and Christopher Nelson
for their early and continued encouragement. How good it is to have Rosemary
Gemperle and Larry Jensen as faithful boosters.

I am happy for all the times together with my granddaughter Helene. A big thank
you to grandsons Alex and Michael for their loving support. Thanks always to
my son Mark and daughter Kirsten for making me proud. Words cannot express
the place of Ron in these poems and in my life—where I am is where we are.

Publisher: Leah Huete de Maines
Editor: Christen Kincaid
Cover Art: J. Ronald Engel
Author Photo: J. Ronald Engel
Cover Design: Elizabeth Maines McCleavy

Order online: www.finishinglinepress.com
        also available on amazon.com

Author inquiries and mail orders:
Finishing Line Press
PO Box 1626
Georgetown, Kentucky 40324
USA

Table of Contents

For you, friends.
These poems are yours now.
I was alone when they appeared.
After the rush of discovery
I longed for you.

Where Things Are

My granddaughter is making a chart:
"Where Things Are"
it's for the summer cottage

placemats flashlight bug spray napkin rings
in the cabinet above the stove
in the dry sink drawer
on a shelf in the coat closet

I am sitting in the orange chair by the window
spruce tree balsam red pine maple
above the cliff edge where the path descends

speaker is placed / located

cookie cutters salad spinner field guides
pie plates puzzles mailbox key
over the fridge on the bookcase
on the wall or check the car

Myrtle Johnson holding our baby daughter ✓
in the scrap book back in Tucson

white haired Myrtle pouring coffee baking whitefish
Milford slack-jawed gutting chub

a ranger and his wife twenty somethings

the moose Milford remembered touching
that moonless night . . . .

Stereopsis

two deer, white tails held high, bound up the road
stop at my neighbor's house to browse

my neighbor does not see them

she left early in the morning for a narrow bed
in a room where nurses come and go
where the hands of a clock tick off the hours

the deer do not see my neighbor

they drop their heads and paw the ground
searching beneath brittle leaves for sustenance

in my mind I see them both

the deer with their long-necked supple curves
my neighbor in a narrow bed, legs twisting side to side
dry leaves, grey-barked sky

clock hands relentlessly circling

After a Phone Call

It is happening.
Our friends are dropping
"like flies" as they say.

Few persons know what that means,
having only seen flies drop
at the end of a swatter.

Not, after a day's drive
and a walk up the fern-sided path,
fumbling for keys in the dark,

and the familiar cedar smell
when the door opens, littering
the floor like spilled raisins.

They haven't seen them
begin to stir at the touch
of a broom, buzz and spin

fruitlessly on their backs
as the dustpan gathers them up,
nor seen them venture

from knot holes where they
braved the winter,
nor watched them, drink in hand,

plummet from the ceiling
in a grand finale,
the chemo having failed.

Cordless

the flowers came up
a voice, my grandson's
exiting plastic
a voice in my hand
in the white white kitchen

the flowers came up
louder this time
as to a senseless infant
or a spider
waiting by the downspout

then I remember
fork-scratched earth
a watering can
streaked legs, pale
seeds like packaged dust

that's great
I say at last
unable to hide
the distance between us

In the Pads of Her Fingers

what to take, that's the question now
packing her bags   resolute   ahead of schedule
some days she'd rather not dwell on it

just lie in bed listening to the flap of a curtain
the mysterious familiar creaks of loose boards
the chirping of birds   their occasional clear whistles

she must add those whistles   tuck them
in a safe corner beside the sighting of that blue
satin back   those blue satin wings

beside returning deer and snow
the first lazy flakes and the paper ones they cut
it's the truth   it's actual   everything

every note in the pads of her fingers
yes   she must layer them with *I'll walk alone*
with lake and sand bar   bare heels

sunk in warm wet   stones mixed
with milky rosaries—
is there room in satin pocket for the plunge

for the curve of her body   rivulets rounding
shoulders and the strength of thigh
muscles   the cooling of her crotch

is there room for that and babies too
for their spittle and puke   their creased buttocks
napkins   should she add the dinner napkins

lace-edged remnants of her mother's handiwork
but how to wrap them so they will not shatter
or even worse   dissolve in tears

what tissue pick to wrap a friend's last handshake
and where to find again the saving jokes
the song sheets   should they rest on top

so the suitcase opens like a music box
or save that place for touch or eyes—
for touch or eyes   and rounded sleep

Query

Before we leave this topic
may I ask:
do you,
like a green leaf
trembling
in an orchard
where peaches exhale
their sweet perfume,
hold
through all tomorrows
a granddaughter's look
clear dewdrop
that flickers
over smooth cheek-hills
touching
igniting?

And will you then
pity—no, not pity—
I mean to say
'erase' erase
completely
the sodden prints
of a man's gray
and thinning hair
bent
over a table, arms
stretched, thumbs
perpendicular—
an exercise said to slow
the aging
that you in cryptic deep
designed?

Not sure what this means

Round this Altar

I. "El Altar," Puerto Morelos, Mexico

Rain-washed stone
stone signed by moss and beetle
sheltering leaves
sea-breathing jungle of
whistling birds
pale
orchids.

To this glen
(stones crusted now and crumbling)
children came
suckled, cried
reached for flashing lizard
laughed
grew tall.

Sun-warmed stone
stone lifted, set in place
cemented, forming
doorways, stairs—
all ruined now, the builders'
names
unknown.

Their tongues like
stone, their tales of kinship
suffering, joy—
stories told in moonlight
'round this altar—
told
no more.

II. Dayton and Fremont Streets, Chicago, late 60s

House-lined streets
streets alive with children—
Polish, African
Mexican
with hula hoops and
fire-
crackers.

Face-bricked streets
streets of stray dogs, straying
entrepreneurs, of
rehabs, rats, fox
stoles and poor folks'
badge:
gray socks.

High-curbed streets
aisles and transepts taverned
coursed by pimp and
plotter—yet commons   *the church?*
filled with sense
of
mission.

Where, one time
street-wise and sheltered found
each other, met
on blooming ground. Guitars
were plucked, fences
stood
ajar.

III. Hyde Park, Chicago, 1995

Snapshots: all
that's left of commons now
streetwalkers' beat:
decanters now;
where clapboard chapels stood
boutiques
shot up.
Shots streaked and
faded. Justice, courage—
See, that's your Grandma, see
beside her Myrtle
thin-faced, strong willed, boxed
in
vellum.

Snapped in his
cleric's garb, your Granddad's waving.
The gray socks lost. The
sheltered organize
on peeled emulsion,
march
in frames.

Shots heard world-
wide reverberate, that was a dreaming
man; he's dead now
Caroline
new shots, new
shoots
break ground.

IV. El Altar

Stone, tree, moss
stone cradle, conduit
of fragments lost
to time, this holy
place, this awe I feel
this
trembling.

Rain-washed stone
stone curb and stoop, evening
and a lighted
hallway, voices
blended, joined
in
protest.

Stone, glass, brick
stone yards adorned with music
child, all this
is gathered up in you
rolled in the sleeping, crystal
heart
of you.

Sun-warmed stone
stone signed by moss and beetle
orange-tipped wing
lizard's crest—
beauty for a moment
for
ever.

A Drawerful of Meadowlarks

on The Field Museum's collection of specimens,
photographed by Terry Evans

1. *Contents*

a drawerful of meadowlarks
two ravens
fifty-four cardinals

great blue heron
folded in half like a yoga master

Eskimo curlew
body straight as a compass
beak to the back of the north wind

red-tailed hawks
tag clear in the Iris print:

killed 7 miles South of Kooper
Nebraska November 5, 1926
Crickets and Snake found in
Stomach Eyes Yellow

twenty photographs acid free
with brown string bound

scrolls of spiderwort
sand bluestem, three-awned grass
coneflowers with haloed heads
(the nimbus stain of drying/dying)

bull snakes coiled in jars
Aunt Maybelle put her piccalilli up in

prairie lizards, carp suckers
boxes of bones, moths, butterflies

a jackrabbit in mid-leap

Plate 20: trumpeter swan
in its bent head the Death of Marat

> cabinet of wonders
> bones and feathers of our ancestors
> gastroliths of creedless space
> with what fear we turn each page
> wait for the rare, the extraordinary
> to surprise our souls

2. *Glossary*

Eastern meadowlark:
family TROOP-ih-al
from habit of gathering
in a large flock or troop

a bird of prairies whose songs
mean spring whose nest
is lined with lespedezas
whose back resembles dried grass

also called common lark
crescent stare, marsh quail
mudlark, medlark, medlar

Eskimo curlew:
one-hundred shot by breakfast

field:
land suitable for tillage

Field Museum, Chicago:

twenty-two million objects
organized in realms
a collection of bird skins
fourth largest in the world
insects occupy two floors

fifty thousand Belizean
neotropical freshwater fishes
recently acquired
while the world rages along,
scientists must still collect

iris: flower, iris: part of the eye
Iris print

prâr'e: noun
as tall as a man on horseback
as far as the eye can see

song comma *birdsong*:
(not represented in the Contents
lost in the case of the curlew
God's ear may hear)

trumpeter swan
once nearly extirpated
its skin made into powder puffs
its call a deep and sonorous
ko ho ko ho

        we wait, our souls
        still capable of wonder
        yet fail to see in these extraordinary
        bones and feathers of our ancestors
        our names upon the page
        our doubts, our tattered space

3. *Historical Background*

a summer's night in 1915
the doctor Bergtold
driving through the canyon dark

observed ahead two small pink spots
reflective eye shine of a night bird

he stopped the car, got out
and fired at the bird
to make certain its identity

Whitman's friend John Burroughs
of a long-legged thrush: *I shot it and saw*
that it was a new acquaintance

I do not believe that anyone
could have shown more zeal

said Darwin *for the most holy cause*
than I did for shooting birds

in 1824 off the Falkland Islands
the ocean covered with foam *like a washing tub*
Scottish naturalist David Douglas
caught on hooks baited with fat pork
forty-nine albatross

their voice like the bleating of goats

after Cyrus Hall McCormick
made a better reaper
he built a factory in Chicago

the increased times
hayfields were mown
led to the meadowlark's decline

within the sunless space
of drawers we file our souls
then turn the page
more than mere wonders
these bones and feathers of our ancestors
a confessional extraordinary

4. *The Photographer*

quail-eyed goddess
who holds in her hand
a prairie that is past

who opens drawer upon drawer
of its mute remains
and stamps her feet in joy

and gratitude for what she finds:
the swaddling clothes
the pattern-revealing outstretched wing

the calligraphy of care that labels demonstrate
affirmation of life in ghastly death

hers a quenchless lust for beauty
a demon need to sing a cradlesong sharp
as blizzarding skies when grasses
crash their cyan cymbals

their yellow black magenta keys

confessional extraordinary
within its margined space
the bloodied trap lines of our ancestors
the tortured longings of our souls
beauty, art, and truth among life's wonders
a billion drops of ink on every page

5. *The Exhibit*

past strollered crowds
museum store, McDonald's *T. rex Sue*

through spirit world of drums and totems
stick figures wearing skulls
beyond but not outside these oceanic shadows
(draw magic circles for your safe return)

a prairie hangs

to its left, Maori meeting house
museum floor its Earth and ceiling Sky
gods and ancestors its walls

and from the TV monitor nearby
there issues forth an incantation
(*the beloved dead
keep company with the living*)
the sweetest, deepest
most sonorous chanting

then wings dipped low I bow
I raise my feathered head
and trumpet to the walls
*ko ho ko ho
allons*

children of the meadowland
ko ho ko ho

> silence drags its feet across the page
> thus all the more extraordinary
> that we, before this cabinet of wonders
> this f-stopped space
> pour forth from deep within our souls
> the sacred music of our ancestors

6. *On Returning Home*

they say the males at sunset
sing facing the sun

chevrons blazoned against gold
they whistle cricket tunes

<u>*earth song*</u> Thoreau called it

I remember how the jars
in my Aunt Mace's cellar
were organized by color
sometimes the jars exploded

blood red shards on sweated walls

we ate the piccalilli
with fresh picked lima beans
that grew beside the hen house

I pushed my hand
beneath the hens' warm bodies
felt for the womb's dread work

we cannot know our ancestors
except as pictures on a page
how can we touch again their joy our souls?
their flame extraordinary?
gastroliths of creedless space
all that remain of wonders

wonders of our ancestors
their extraordinary space
and our souls on every page

Close to the Border

I don't look, I just shoot,
she says, pointing her bazooka-like lens
      at a Black-Chinned combatant
      dive-bombing a sweet-water tank.

Couple from Dallas—she blogs
hummingbirds exclusively—
      he's into petrochemicals;
      it's their first time in the Huachucas.

Our first time too in this hummer hotspot
with its steep lush canyons
      close to the Mexican border,
      close to where Geronimo surrendered.

We talk over the rat-a-tat of frames
being advanced; our new friends are into
      zoom talk, f-this and
      f-that, autofocus on, off.

Nearby Fort Huachuca is
where they're going next; we tell them
      what the guidebook says—stay off the grass,
      avoid stumbling on live ammunition.

We're sitting on lawn chairs
in a local birder's yard; our cars are parked
      behind our backs and a dozen
      numbered feeders hang from trees

or protrude from dusty soil
like poison mushrooms.
      At a certain angle of the late afternoon sun
      the males' throat-armor flashes.

On the way here we saw a blimp,
one of several deployed to support
        the whirlybird copters
        of the U.S. Border Patrol.

They say it can read a newspaper,
a smuggler or an immigrant.
            Female Anna on Number Seven
            a birder calls . . .

. . . .

I miss it, deep in thought, seeing instead
the gold-feathered flare of a Prothonotary Warbler
        that descended from a glass sky
        I lay face up on canoe struts

skimming shadows long ago; remembering too
from deep inside a cattail marsh
        the descending cry of a Sora, a wail
        that runs down your gut to your toes . . .

. . . .

They've got one, the Texan shouts,
pointing to a green and white chopper
        circling above us;
        by 'one' he means

a border-crosser caught
 before that unlucky soul reached
        the water jug. We rise
        and watch it dip from sight.

. . . .

Betty Crocker Yellow Cake Mix,
Pennzoil, Vernors, Aunt Jemima
        Blue-Throated, Magnificent, Black-
        Chinned, Rufous—sitting in a booth

at Papa's Diner we review the birds we saw;
a pair of broad-shouldered boys,
        one blond, one copper-skinned,
        dressed in boots and Desert Storm fatigues

are buying candy bars to take back to the Fort—
clean shaven, innocent, as innocent as I was
        when homeland was the same as home,
        they joke and slap each other on the back.

Leaving Indiana

Today with a wind from the northwest
Lake Superior moving in ceaseless broken lines
the sky a pale blue tinged with yellow
and a sharp horizon line, I can think about it
how the blood root had taken hold
its creamy petals held in prayer-clasped leaves
how the Dutchman's breeches with their
filmy carroty foliage were spreading
how the trillium had found its dappled sun.

I can let myself remember days of searching
for their likeness, cruising back roads
where I'd seen them blooming, noting signs
of imminent upheaval—plastic ribbons tied to stakes,
tree trunks spotted orange, a backhoe at the ready.
And I'd ask the owners sweetly if they minded,
could I make a few excisions?
They always answered, *not a problem.*
Take what you want, we're busy here.

And as I spaded around the roots of liver-lobed
hepatica, of glowing wood anemone,
plants that white-haired Barbara Plampin
pointed out on walks beside the Little Calumet
annual messengers of an exuberance
dwelling beneath mud-splashed soil
I'd condemn the builders of that tennis court or circle drive
and count the growing bags of orphan children
crowded in the back seat of the car.

Today, while sun and icy wind play Crazy Eights
the cabin porch too cold for sitting, its cushions
too intensely yellow to remain inside, my thoughts
go south a long day's drive to my former Duneland home.
Memories surface, hopes for that low spot I'd chosen
that protected saucer, sheltered by witch hazel

how I'd dig each cozy pocket, fill the holes
with water from a hose, then lift the dangled
roots and crudely stuff the rescued in.

In wintry March with snowmelt forming runnels
and returning migrants testing out their calls
I'd finish filling all four feeders, wish the chickadees
good day, then walk on wobbly broken stones and search
for signs of what I'd planted months before.
They didn't all do well, squirrels dug them up
some died of trauma, some bloomed
profusely for a season then left dissatisfied
unable in the end to relinquish what they'd had.

Uncertainty added to the drama
and with the first discovered bud I'd run inside
To yell *guess what!* and organize a tour.
Instantly the hollow spot and all the paupered
neighboring surround, all garlic mustard, weeds and briar
became a flowered rug, a carpet purchased
from no retail store, blossoms from no catalogue
became the variegated flooring of the Dunes
before the plow, the mills, before my house.

The blood root was a hideaway, a plant
I hadn't known I'd planted that just appeared.
Ten years at least before it felt at home.
Yet, even after months of drought
there would be one or two, first flowers to emerge.
They never lasted long; if the wind were fierce
as it often was, they were defrocked by noon.
The month we sold the house they'd made it up the hill.
Blood root, rooted blood, rejoicing in the sunshine.

Now that I have joined the ranks of jilting lovers
who, even if our fate no longer matters
to those left stranded by our leaving

since they must find their own solutions
flourish or decline, no thanks to what we
obviously aren't doing, I ask to be remembered
by the universe as well as by its humans
who are capable of good, who also
may be moving, who must find their beauty elsewhere.

Lifetime Memberships

ah Len my friend, the leaf you cut
 the one you held to my face
  your blue eyes audacious
   asking *what does it taste like?*

we were in Cairns outside a pasty shop
  strange greeting we had traveled so far
  what does it taste like? *like leaf* I answered
   flirting *it tastes like leaf*

when we stepped from a cramped
 Land Rover into fresh forested air
  I got credit for sighting the male
   Cairns Birdwing, fluttering high in the canopy

you said of the day ahead *she's beaut*
 she's apples you said of the trees *smooth*
  equals gum rough equals box bumps equal bloodroot
   Let us not be tourists in this land

night cries of scrubfowl chowchillas
 at dawn palms like the rising sun
  get the death adders out of your pocket and pay up
   leaf was not the answer celery was

. . . .

almost all that I remember of the Grand Canyon
  is the twenty minute wait to use the women's restroom
   Arkansas has license plates that feature
    an ivory-billed woodpecker

. . . .

consider Butterfly Haven   where hundreds of butterflies fly freely
alighting on fragrant flowering plants
for your child's birthday party
lifetime memberships available

although the excessive humidity
    has its drawbacks   the flitting sprites
        excite my granddaughter who kneels
            as one alights on a fragrant flowering plant

while I examine a pale paisley pair
  copulating   and learn from the guide
      that their eggs   though fertile
        will never be laid

Butterfly Haven has selected plants
  the larvae cannot digest
    the female will hold the eggs in her abdomen
        rather than subject her young to starvation

.   .   .   .

we danced to Waltzing Matilda
    I was awkward out of step
        later you called from the fan palms
        and I found you

shock of white hair   salmon-colored shirt
    arms around a giant cycad—
        dinosaur of the plant world
            from a time before flowers

I should have said celery
    because everything has a flavor   a taste
      like a man   like a woman

        ah Len my friend—
          can you see it   taste it still?

Beneath Sofa Cushions

No, I didn't find
beneath the sofa cushions,
that recipe for sugar-dusted crullers
your grandmother made
the Tuesday before Lent

nor the ring
I never should have sold
with the oval turquoise stone
and band worn thin
against my mother's finger

I didn't find my father's meerschaum pipe
the one I broke and carefully replaced—
that was before your cashmere sweater
left hanging on a classroom chair
and prior to the pale green one

that clung suggestively
you maybe can't remember now—
at any rate it wasn't there.
I didn't find "Open the Door, Richard"
you will be pleased to know

but the Brandenburg Concertos—
do they still make Christmas
in the Calvert Street apartment?
guess they're in some dusky
store with metronomes.

No body parts showed up,
no blood-stained underpants
~~can you believe I miss them~~? *Did I miss them*
~~well I do~~, no peels of sunburned flesh
or the afterbirths I never saw.

The flowers that I picked
and pocketed
intending to attach their names
were not lodged beneath the cushions
nor were their names nearby.

I didn't find the wood smoke,
powdered Tang, the bonding charge
of bourbon, books we read—
~~not one of these.~~
Just crumbs

from a muffin that you served me
with our morning coffee,
crumbs I gather singly
in my open palm,
careful not to spill.

Vespers

Abide with me
her voice a thin cracked reed
suds coursing down her arm
and I am drying
cups of dimestore willow pattern
stacking wobbly pairs on the oilcloth-
covered table

Fast falls the eventide
her voice a thin cracked reed
her apron wet above
a shapeless dress, old lady shoes
outside the curtained window
roses soak in shadow
lights go on across the alley

dismissed
to do my homework
I rush upstairs to my room
she hangs her apron
on the hook inside the pantry door
The darkness deepens,
Lord with me abide.

Picking Berries Again

my granddaughter and I
walk the dusty road

    a butterfly
        black with an ivory sash
            a royal V across its opened wings

alights   waits for our shadows to come close   floats

repeats and repeats

    until finally
        tiring of this catch- me- if- you- can-

    stops   and   suns

    while we examine the frayed edge of a wing

blueberry beads dot low green foliage
        too low to bend without an ache

and so I too stand unmoving

with thoughts of summers to come

        a pied piper in new satin frockcoat

    the child grown woman

and who will pick the berries then?

Notes

Cover—Bloodroot (*Sanguinaria canadensis*). Photo taken of newly emerged plant in our garden.

"In the Pads of her Fingers"—playing an upright piano and swimming in Lake Michigan were among Ann Wheat's favorite activities; the poem was written during her long illness.

"Round this Altar"—written on the birth of Caroline, granddaughter of Mary Lou and Neil Shadle. Neil, with Ron Engel, Dick Brown, and other residents of the Ranch Triangle neighborhood, founded the Neighborhood Commons, an interracial community organization.

"A Drawerful of Meadowlarks" refers to: (1) *From Prairie to Field: Photographs by Terry Evans,* The Field Museum, 2002, an exquisite cardboard-bound book; (2) The Field Museum of Natural History in Chicago and its collection of plant and animal remains, among which are the prairie specimens chosen by Evans; and (3) the Pacific Spirits gallery of the Field Museum, at the time of the writing of the poem located adjacent to the Evans exhibit.

    The quote from Darwin is from *The Autobiography of Charles Darwin*, ed. by Nora Barlow (New York: W.W. Norton, 1958). The eyeshine incident that led Dr. Bergtold to shoot a poor-will is recorded in *The Audubon Society Encyclopedia of North American Birds* by John K. Terres (New York: Alfred A. Knopf, 1980). The quote from John Burroughs is from *Wake Robin* (1871). The line, "we wait for the rare and the extraordinary to surprise our souls" is from *Wonders and the Order of Nature, 1150-1750* by Katherine Park, Zemurray Stone, and Lorraine Dastore (Zona Books, 1998).

    'Gastroliths' are small stones swallowed by some birds, reptiles, and fish to aid digestion. The chorus to the poem forms a sestina.

"Close to the Border"—*avoid stumbling on live ammunition* is printed in a guidebook to birding at Fort Huachuca. Apparently, monsoon rains periodically unearth unexploded ammunition.

"Lifetime Memberships" recalls one of several trips to Queensland, Australia in the company of Len Webb, recipient of many honors for his pioneering rainforest research, and his partner Doris, a dear friend.

No single locale or lifetime vocation defines poet **Joan Gibb Engel**. Born in a middle-class suburb of Baltimore, she has lived in a Chicago neighborhood torn by racial strife and poverty as well as in economically secure and biologically rich Indiana Dunes. For several summers she and her husband and their two children lived on an isolated island within Isle Royale National Park. They now divide their time between the city of Tucson and the wooded environment of Michigan's Upper Peninsula, this latter a cherished place of longest tenure.

A graduate of Goucher College with a degree in biology, she taught art in middle school for many years and for a time became a potter. She participated with her husband in a push for housing justice, earned a PhD in English from the University of Illinois at Chicago and, before turning to poetry, edited several books and wrote non-fiction essays.

Her poems have appeared in numerous journals including *The American Journal of Poetry, Cutthroat, Canary Journal, Comstock Review, San Pedro River Review,* and *Under a Warm Green Linden.*

To the heady joy of working with persons of diverse races and economic situations is the happiness she finds in nature's beauty. In a repeated memory Joan walks beside the Little Calumet among wood anemone, Dutchman's breeches, trillium, and a carpet of spring ephemerals. This happiness, however, comes with a fear borne of centuries of ill-treatment of the planet and the fervent wish that the future may bring wisdom to humankind, and healing to wounded Earth.